**Be true
to yourself**

FIESTA
of HAPPINESS

Be true
to yourself

David Baird

Andrews McMeel
Publishing

Kansas City

Introduction

In authenticity there is truth.
So it should become obvious . . .
That to be ourselves,
We should strive to be true to ourselves.
These days—
Peer pressures, high-flying careers,
Advertising, marketing, fashion, and spin—
We seem oddly compelled
To be anything but true.
Anything but ourselves!
We struggle to fit into the latest styles,
We work too hard,
We decorate and redecorate
Guided by half-hour television design gurus,

And seek out perfect partners
Via the Internet.
In truth, few of us
Are near to being true to ourselves.
But relax. Celebrate . . .
For there is truth in authenticity.
If we can somehow become content
With being who we actually are
We will find that authenticity
And with it . . . truth!
And when we can be true to ourselves,
Well . . .
In the end,
That's what people will remember about us.

Start as you mean to go on

Every day should be a fiesta.

Put on your glad rags and be glad to be alive.

Start the day by greeting yourself . . .

Pamper yourself,

Be friendly to yourself.

You're a star.

You're special.

Allow yourself to feel good being with you

And others will, too.

Treasure today

Say to yourself:
"Today I am.
I vibrate with passion
And the rhythm of my life has sent
All sadness into exile.
From my first waking breath
I am . . .
I am!
Listen to my beat.
I am amazing.
And today is
My Day!"

Join in

The sidelines are for spectators;
The real play is up there on the stage.
The whole world's the stage
And everyone has a role to play.
If you're not certain of your lines
Just improvise for a while
And you'll soon be word perfect.
One thing is for certain:
The moment you make your entrance
You'll become part of a great drama,
So big and intriguing,
You'll wonder why
You didn't join the cast before.

Cultivate happiness

Each of us is given a garden
Called life.
Plant in it the seed of your ability,
And enjoy watching it grow.
Keep it fertilized
With your thoughts
And watered with your imagination.
From time to time pick
A beautiful, fragrant bouquet of happiness.
For yourself and those around you.

Water your spirit

Take a spell of R & R,
(That's rest and relaxation).
Why hold your breath
Hesitating on the water's edge?
Come on in; the water's warm.
Recreation equals delight,
So let the world fade away delightfully
As you float in your daydream pool.
Then dive to the bottom . . . and come up . . .
With a pearl
Beyond price.

Make your mark

Ever since man began his trek through life
His prime desire has been to leave his mark
For posterity.
Some have had great monuments built to honor them,
Some create great industries or estates.
Others have quite simply touched a heart or two along the way . . .
But for that they'll never be forgotten.

Dance with a difference

Why not
Dance to a different beat,
Create a stir,
Go faster, higher, harder, longer?
When you find yourself out of step with everyone else,
Just listen to the rhythm beating deep within your heart
And move in time to your own tune.

Subscribe to life

Take a look around you
And see who is truly
Taking part in life.
It's amazing how many people
Don't get the point of it all
And go through each day
Resigned to miss out while others live.
Anyone can join in at any time.
Don't wait to be invited—
Just take a deep breath and jump right in.

Dance to the rhythm

Each new day has its own rhythms.

We can either work against them and accept the consequences,

Or we can go with them . . .

Use them correctly and they'll serve you well.

Listen, feel that pulse.

There's no point waltzing to the twist.

So let those muscles go, go, go!

Ease the tension out of your body

And sway to the beat of the day.

Don't squander your energies trying to tango

Against the tempo of the new day.

Always remember that,

Man masters nature, not with force

But by understanding its ways and respecting its rhythms.

Sing a song

Compose the song of your day . . .
Your moment . . . your world . . . your life.
Australian Aborigines have their song lines
To help them navigate through their lands,
Each made up of stories based on tribal legends
From the Dreamtime.
Why not wake up and go on a walkabout!
Discover your legends, your dreams, and your truths.
Put them all together in your song
And add to it day by day.
To go through life singing another's song line
Is nothing less than enslavement.
Choose freedom
And travel your own song line.

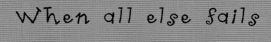

When all else fails

When all else fails we always have ourselves
To fall back on.
Make a contract with yourself
For now and for the rest of your days
Never to let yourself down
And from that moment,
Travel onward through your life
Safe in the knowledge that
No matter what happens
There is always someone
You can depend on . . .
And that's
You!

Don't tread water

Treading water is for the fat old fish
At the bottom of the stream, who just
Lies there facing the current,
Going nowhere.
If you feel you're getting nowhere fast
Why spend your life treading water
Waiting for progress?
There can be no real progress except
In yourself and by yourself.
So get those fins working
And find your best stroke.
Glide gracefully
Through life's waters,
Whether they're calm or troubled.

Dare to be great

Why not?
No matter how small something that you
Achieve may seem,
See its greatness and others will, too.
How great is a grain of sand?
Take a multitude of them
And you can have a beach . . .
An island . . . a continent!
No achievement is too small
To be considered great—
A child's first unaided steps,
A word uttered,
A thought,
A project . . .
A life.

Mirror image

Want to change your image?
Then start with the way you behave.
The way we act is the mirror in which we show our image.
Just as the looking glass lets you know you exist by showing you yourself,
Framed and behind glass,
In an unreal place of reflection, so
You, here on the living side of the glass,
Must let yourself know that you exist and are really needed.

You are.
We all are.
We all contribute to the worldview,
We're all essential to the big picture.
So reflect on that!

The book of life

Who wants someone else to write their life story?
Pen a memo to yourself:
"I am the author of my own life.
Today it will be a comedy and not a tragedy.
I shall look out for the humor and opportunity in every situation,
From the moment I rise to the close of my day.
I will live so that I would have no dismay
In going through the same life again
From beginning to end . . .
Except, perhaps, for a few corrections
To the next edition."

Take care of your bodywork

Aren't they great? Bodies?

No two the same.

Each a unique vessel taxiing us around.

And just like a limousine or a classic car, if you

Treat it with a little tender loving care

It will run smoothly for a lifetime.

Today, think this:

"This is my body,

And I will not allow anyone to tinker with it in a way

I do not choose and I won't let anyone or anything

Make me feel bad about it.

My bodywork is my own business!"

On top of the world

Stand still and let the great outdoors
Stimulate your senses.
You don't need to turn to anything else.
There's color in the hedgerows,
Sound on the mountaintops,
Flavors in the wind.
Nature in her divine diversity bestows
All the tools and materials,
Inspiration and incentive for us all to lead
Creative and fulfilling lives.
The very best high there is
Is to feel yourself standing on the top of the world
With its beauty laid out before you.

The art of life

Pluck up your Picasso
And start to flash your Monet around.
What is art and what is not art?
Can we think of ourselves as art?
There is art in everything we do and the way we do it.
Don't dwell upon what you can't do
And leave undone what you can do.
So much stress is caused by people
Taking on what they don't understand.
If you want to feel happy,
Do something you can do well
And celebrate your talent and the pleasure it gives.
The essence of all art is to delight in giving pleasure.
The Mona Lisa knew that . . .

Be influential

Find out just how easy it is
To influence your fellow human beings.
Hum a well-known tune throughout the day
And chances are you'll hear it echoing
In the voices of others
Without their even realizing.
If you're not afraid to show your enthusiasm,
And you believe in what you do,
Then others less certain
Will dare to turn off a route of trepidation
And travel life's superhighway.

Pump up the power

Now's the time to switch off all feelings
Of being powerless.
Power lies welling up inside of all of us,
Too often unused
While around us power is abused
And wrongs go unrighted.
You have the power to say no.
Choose to use your individual power
For good and happiness will prevail.

Choices

Yes no yes no yes no?
Red blue?
Yes red, no blue?
No red, yes no?
In out, up down?
Do don't, can can't?
Choices sit on the shelf like
New shoes in a shoe shop.
If the in crowd are squeezing into a must-have shoe
And the one pair left are too tiny for you
Don't feel compelled into choosing them
If you're really a size 9, buy that size.

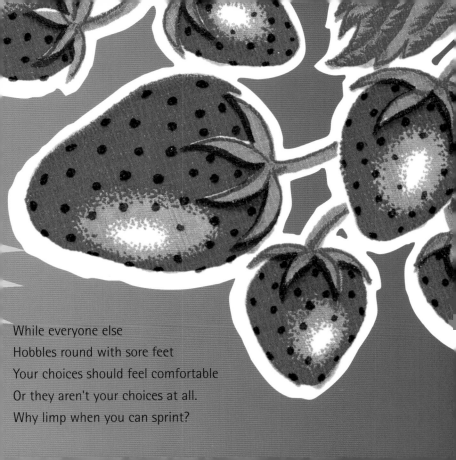

While everyone else
Hobbles round with sore feet
Your choices should feel comfortable
Or they aren't your choices at all.
Why limp when you can sprint?

Rumor

Rumor has it
That you are fantastic
And are really going places . . .
That your life is exciting
And you really know how to live.
That's the sort of rumor
We'd all like to have circulating about us.
Well, the only way to achieve it
Is by living up to it.

How do you feel?

Hey, what others think doesn't matter.
You can be who you are and say what you feel.
Do what feels right to you,
In your heart.
Look out at life with your own eyes.
Live! Soar!
Why?
Because so few of us ever accomplish in our lifetime
All that we feel lies within us,
But it's when we touch our true core and let it
Guide us that we release
Our infinite potential.
The people who matter
Will be glad you're following your own instincts.

How do I look?

Ditch the mirror and take a good long look inside yourself today.

Look into your heart

And your vision will soon become clear.

Why not just be yourself?

You will discover your inner strength.

Hear yourself proclaim:

"I am myself,

I am proud of who and what I am!"

Feel yourself awaken as you look inside

And make yourself this promise:

"I am just going to be myself."

Chances are you'll be mistaken for someone famous!

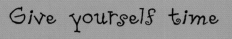

Give yourself time

Are you losing touch with the events of your life?
Well, stake your claim to them quickly
If you want to direct your life.
Spend time finding out who you really are.
Then relax and be more of that.
Fearlessly be yourself!
There is, after all, only one you—for all time.
You are more than you realize,
More than you can ever define.
But don't overdo the analyzing—
The more time you spend trying to pin down
The definition, the less time you'll have to spend living.

Finding meaning

Stop running round like a headless chicken
Searching for the meaning of life.
Stand still and look at what's going on
And what gives meaning to your life.
What is it that lies behind your
decisions?
Can you back them up with your heart?
As the whole world dashes by, muttering:
"What's it all about? What's it all about?"
Turn your own mantra into:
"It's about living! It's about me!"

Be your leading light

Never forget that you are your own leader.
If you do not choose to lead yourself,
You will forever be led by others.
Throughout your life you will face many challenges
And your attitude will determine
Where and how you will end up.
You can choose to avoid the things that frighten you
And blend into the rest of the crowd.
Or you can overcome your fears
And choose to make a difference.
Touch the sky!
No one else should take the lead role
In your life—it was written for you.

Laughter effects

Don't stifle your emotions.
Never be afraid to use and display
Your sense of humor
Even the most dangerous moments in life
Can have their humorous side.
In a tense situation humor is a calming perfume.
Today, do something humorous.
Anyone can frown—
It takes courage to be a clown.

Just be you

In a world that seems as if it is doing its utmost
To make you anyone else but you,
Stand firm.
Cherish your individuality,
Your strength,
Your ability to stand out from the crowd.
Never hand over your individuality to others
Or take yourself for granted
Be yourself and no one but yourself.

Sleep easy

"To sleep perchance to dream . . ."
Dream of the person you'd like to be,
And make that the person you are!
Learn to live,
And live to the fullest.
At night, after soaring,
Let go of doubts, of fears, of worries
Before lying down to sleep.
Relax and dream your dream.
With peace of mind,
You will get more sleep
And wake next day
To enjoy yourself.

Challenge your senses

Our senses are our doors and windows
On this world.
But doors can creak and windows get grimy,
Through lack of care.
Not protecting our senses
Is like trying to sail through a storm in a rudderless ship.
So tend your senses carefully,
Mend, retune, and renew them to
Perfect working order.

Today focus on sight,
Tomorrow listen with heightened care,
The next day separate out each smell . . .
Then notice how the skies seem bluer,
The wind keener,
And the sea air tangier.

Set the pace

Adopt the pace of nature; her secret is patience.
Why should we be in such desperate hurry
To succeed?
You cannot rush an apple tree to mature.
It will stand untiringly, through all weathers,
And quietly resolve itself to bear fruit.
With calm minds, we cannot be perplexed or frightened.
We can go forward in fortune or misfortune
At the right pace for us, if we keep in step with ourselves.
Steer clear of the "dizzied-by-progress" folk—
Their speed exceeds their ability to succeed.
In your own time, your own life
Can be brought to perfection.

High days and holidays

Happiness comes and goes.

We all have periods of gloom.

When we wonder whether the good times

Will ever return.

Why do we limit our capacity for fun to just

A few short seasons?

Why not instead make every day a holiday

And revel in living.

Celebrate your friends and the happiness they bring into your life.

Celebrate being a giving person.

Apply yourself to work that you enjoy

And every day can seem like a holiday.

But beware, none of us could stand a lifetime of unbroken ecstasy.

There will be downs, but with so much to look forward to

We can learn to manage them a little better!

Hear no evil

Don't be led through life by your ears!
We tend to hear what we want to hear and
Disregard the rest.
So be on guard,
Always balance credulity with common sense,
And never allow untruths
To become the foundation blocks
On which your life is built.
Remember the best you have found in others
And give them the benefit of the doubt.

Because of you

Let yesterday go
And begin to live this day.
Your past is not your identity.
You, living now, is your identity.
Because of you countless thousands will have their place
In a chain of events that would not otherwise exist,
Just as a butterfly flapping its wings in Japan
Can set off a hurricane in New York.
Because you're you, a cat may purr or a life may be saved.
There will be smiles
And laughter
And joy.
You are more than you know.

Find time

When was the last time you thought to yourself:
"One day I'll get around to making my life a little better"?
And how often do you put off doing just that?
To deny this hunger is no different from denying actual hunger.
Would you put off eating until you die of starvation?
Make time for yourself!
If you want time, you must make it.
No matter how busy you think you are
Cancel or postpone some chores and
Surrender yourself to yourself.
You'll gain from the things in life you enjoy.
If you feel you cannot make time for recreation you will
soon be obliged to make time for illness.

Elect to select

From the moment you wake and get out of bed
To the moment you return there,
You have option upon option to be selective about.
Shall I drag myself wearily from these sheets or

Leap into the day?
Shall I brush and floss . . . or neither?
What shall I wear; what shall I eat?
Walk or ride . . . ?
Eat in or eat out . . . ?
Apply myself, or just tread water . . . ?
Sink or swim, it's up to you.
Seek entertainment or retreat to solitude.
The only reason that you are not
Skipping down the High Street
In a pair of flippers and a diving mask,
Singing "Ying Tong Tiddle Aye Po"
Is because your selections for this day
Have made it so.

Dedicate a day to yourself

It's Me Day today!
A year has all sorts of holidays and anniversaries,
Birthdays and big days.
But resolve to set aside one day in your year
Specifically to celebrate just being you.
To reward yourself for what you've achieved,
For cresting the waves and climbing the hills.
A day no one else will organize,
A day you design and conduct
And where the only presents received are the ones
You buy for yourself.
Twenty-four hours of self-pampering.
When anything goes.

Celebrate life

At whatever stage of life you are,
Just setting out or nearing the end,
Remember to celebrate living.
There's a lot to celebrate.
Yourself.
Sing yourself.
Praise yourself.
Tell yourself how glad you are
To be
You.

Let off steam

It's no good bottling everything up inside.
Any physicist will tell you that energy confined is
An explosion in waiting.
But when it's transformed into something else
It really becomes interesting.
Steam turns the turbine that creates the electricity
That powers infinite other applications.
It's no good trying to let off steam when you're only lukewarm—
You've got to be on the boil.
But once you are, anything is possible
If you let yourself go.

In focus

If you're going to minimize anything in your life,
Make it your problems.
Confine them to the viewfinder in the mind's camera
And edit them out of your life movie.
Your life movie is a big-screen presentation
Shot in glorious technicolor
And what you see on that screen depends upon
What you choose to focus on along the way.
When you reach the closing titles your film will be
"In the Can" and not the cannot!

Pause and reflect

Now and then, it's a good thing
To pause for a few moments in
Our pursuit of happiness and just be happy.
Don't waste these precious moments of
Pause and reflection dwelling upon
What might have been and on missed chances.
We can learn to know ourselves by
The actions we choose to take
Following pause and after reflection.
Only then will we know what is in us.

A fruitful life

Accept others:
Their looks, no matter how strange to you—
You look just as strange to them;
Their behavior, regardless of how puzzling they may seem—
As ours must be equally puzzling to them;
Their beliefs—
Accept them just as you would have them accept yours.
If mutual, such acceptance will dispel anger, fear, and resentment
And bring about inner peace and tranquillity
In a vast and varied orchard,
Each of us is a tree that our beliefs grow on.
So have belief in yourself and respect the beliefs of others—
And enjoy a fruitful life.

Be reasonable

Do you ask too much of yourself?
Make unreasonable demands?
You can't be everything to everyone,
Be everywhere at once.
A rope pulled too taut will snap,
So cut yourself some slack.
Accept yourself, loosen up . . .
And you'll have a string of successes.

Ask and you will receive

Who said you can't teach an old dog new tricks?
Watch a child today,
And notice how many times it asks Why?
Why is there a sun?
Why is the sky blue?
Why do bees buzz?
And why can't we have ice cream before pizza?
Why indeed?
Life is filled with questions.
Even if we can't find or don't like the answers
Nothing in our life alters if the questions within us
Go unasked.

Imagineer

Someone thought up space travel
And someone else came up with computers.
A person just like me invented the car and
Another dreamed up the yo-yo.
Close your eyes.
What do you see?
What do you wish to see?
Imagine the world's biggest, fastest,
And most thrilling roller coaster.
Design it in your mind's eye and then take it for a test ride.
Construct the palace of your dreams or
The newest solution to global communication.
If you can imagineer it,
Then it is probably possible.
Dare to make it so.

The whole truth

Truth is a source of happiness
Waiting for you at that place where your true self is
Longing to be discovered.
Truth brings about confidence.
You can be anything you allow yourself to be—
That's the challenge.
That's the opportunity!
The most difficult part of any opportunity
Is taking the first step,
Making the first decision.
And that, my friend, is up to
You!

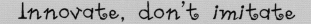

Innovate, don't imitate

Why go through life trying to be like somebody else
When you haven't lived being you?
Why spend time trying to achieve what others have
Already achieved when you could achieve so much else?
Imagine a racehorse wanting to be a bicycle,
A Chihuahua pretending to be a German Shepherd
It's ridiculous! Preposterous! you say.
Be glad to be one of a kind,
Rejoice in who and what you are, and in what you can do.
That's the mark of a true original.

One careful driver

Along the way, while you're celebrating your own
Wonderful existence
Be careful not to run down
Anyone else.
Think of life as a two-way street.
An uncaring person is a vehicle out of control,
An accident just waiting to happen.
To become a caring person you must take on board the
Responsibility of caring not just for yourself, but also for others.
Give right of way, and
Don't hog the road.
Take care to care.

The greatest journey imaginable

Jump aboard.
Take a trip around the world every single day!
Think about it—each and every day we are riding upon this vast globe,
Imagining ourselves to be standing still . . .

Or getting nowhere when, in fact, we are

Hurtling through space and rotating a full 360 degrees

Every twenty-four hours—a dizzying notion.

Let the notion take hold of you and the next time you

Stare up at the stars, you'll be able to feel you are

Part of it all,

Part of the universe . . .

Part of the infinite . . .

And embarked upon

The greatest journey imaginable!

Give yourself a hand

By all means, enjoy being admired!
While you stand up there in the limelight, taking your bows and
Bathing in the warmth of the ovation you receive from others,
Consider whether you have a life
Away from that place, from that moment.
Make sure that once the light goes off
And you find yourself back in the everyday world
You can draw as much strength from the applause
That you give to yourself.
Or do you only exist when others applaud?
It's all right to raise the admiration of others, but it's
Essential to find it in yourself if you are to enjoy
Happiness.
Now, give yourself a hand!

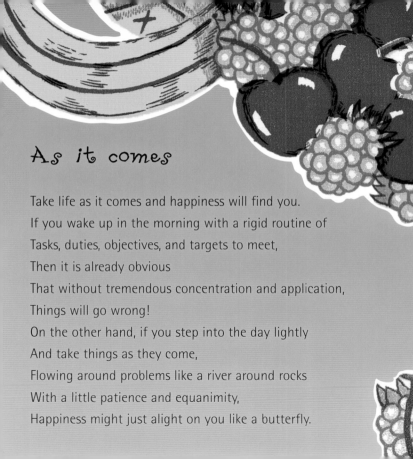

As it comes

Take life as it comes and happiness will find you.
If you wake up in the morning with a rigid routine of
Tasks, duties, objectives, and targets to meet,
Then it is already obvious
That without tremendous concentration and application,
Things will go wrong!
On the other hand, if you step into the day lightly
And take things as they come,
Flowing around problems like a river around rocks
With a little patience and equanimity,
Happiness might just alight on you like a butterfly.

Sow the seed of happiness

At times, when you just can't seem to find the essential ingredients for
Your own happiness, go out into the world and
Bask in the happiness of others.
Examine it closely, and you will discover that it is often
The simplest things that can trigger happiness.
Recognize this, and you will have learned that
Even a single seed that you plant in a pot can bring you endless joy.

First published by **MQ Publications Limited**
12 The Ivories, 6-8 Northampton St., London, N1 2HY

Copyright © 2003 MQ Publications Limited
Text © 2003 **David Baird**
Design: **Balley Design Associates**

ISBN: 0-7407-3538-1

Library of Congress Control Number on file